20/20 Leadership Lessons
Seeing Visions and Focusing on Reality

Dr. Cedrick Bridgeforth

DEDICATION

To the loving memory of two of my biggest fans
who joined the great cloud of witnesses

Vanessa Gill

Tanae M. Robinson

2020LeadershipLessons.org

ACKNOWLEDGMENTS

This work would not have been possible without the editorial support of Dr. Charles P. Loeb, the backbone of Peggy Loeb, the encouragement of Dr. Sherry Daniels, and the unconditional love of BLD. The love and care of those I know as family and friends has sustained me. Your belief in me has pushed me beyond the limitations I set in my own mind. Thank you for believing in me.

INTRODUCTION

When I was in 10th Grade I was enrolled in a typing class. In fact, I was the only male in that class and there were some who looked upon me with great suspicion for choosing typing versus woodshop. After a few weeks in the class, I began to realize I develop an excruciating headache every day during typing class. I informed my teacher and she questioned whether I needed glasses or not. She explained that the type of reading we were doing would often expose weakened eyesight. I told my mom about the headaches and the teacher's inquiry and within a few days I was sitting in an optometrists office getting what I believe was my first eye exam. I walked out of the office with a prescription for my first pair of glasses.

I had been walking around with the ability to see but I could not focus as well or as quickly as I could with the help of corrective lenses. The same is true of leaders who lack a clear vision of where they are going or where they are leading others. They can see some things and they can make out what is before them, but they cannot focus well or quickly because they do not have a clear vision of what is ahead. Therefore, they cannot devise and implement a sustainable plan for how to get there.

This book is for leaders and leadership open to seeing more clearly. This process will work best if the reader first admits: "I need to see more clearly so I can focus on the vision." Within this book the concept of 20/20 Leadership will emerge and come into view with each reading, each prayer, and every journal entry. You may be tempted to skip the journaling, but I strongly caution against that because there is great power in your words. By writing your initial or latent thoughts on each subject or attribute, you are creating a path from where you are in your current thoughts to where you must be in pursuit of a vision as a 20/20 leader.

20/20 Leadership is rooted in a truth that the leader must see the vision in order to lead others toward it as they develop their own 20/20 Leadership. This model is perpetual and collaborative in nature because the best leaders are those who instill confidence and inspire others to act and to advance shared values for the sake of the mission. The mission is in constant service of the vision. It is the vision that motivates 20/20 Leadership to inspire others to see what can be and to move in that direction.

Leadership is a word in maximum rotation in the English language but its attributes and effect seem to be in short supply in most arenas of life. It can also be stated that leadership and leading are not interchangeable. It cannot be assumed that because a person is in a leadership role, by virtue of title or position that the person is leading.

There are several modifiers offered to seek clarity and to draw categorical distinctions between leaders. We read about servant leaders, principled leaders, disciplined leaders, and transformational leaders to name a few. In addition there are many blogs, books and sites dedicated to effective leadership, nonprofit leadership, entrepreneurial leadership, and transactional leadership. Some distinctions are helpful but in the end, if the person or persons charged to lead do not have the nerve and the gall to lead, leadership will come from wherever it needs to come from to accomplish the agreed upon mission.

It is my hope that by engaging leaders from many stations of life and in various sectors of society in the art of reading, contemplating, praying and journaling that more individuals will discover, hone and actualize their leadership gifts by leading themselves in more intentional practices and inspiring others to seek a vision of what is inside and in store for them, as well.

20/20 Leadership is based on a principle that leadership is most effective and sustainable when there is a clearly stated vision that is pursued with absolute focus on the mission at-hand. A bias imbedded in the reflective questions, confessions and prayers found in this book is that leadership is a gift and leading is a privilege.

This book was not written as one continuous narrative. Instead the premise is that each chapter contains several attributes, characteristics or behaviors of leaders that are to be examined one at a time. That may be accomplished in solitude, with an accountability partner or small group. There are many quotations, musings and scriptures included as prompts to guide you as you consider what it is to see the visions God has for you, your family and your organization while focusing on reality and seeking clarity of vision.

Whatever you do

Work at it with all your heart

As if working for the Lord

And for no one else.

-My daily mantra based on Colossians 3:23

It took about two weeks for me to actually receive my new glasses. I left school early to go pick them up. The doctor placed them on my face and spun the chair so I could look at myself in the mirror. He did that before he performed the necessary exam to ensure I could see correctly. Looking into the mirror was powerful because I was in clear view of my self. Then, when I looked through the exam apparatus I could see what had been tiny dots two weeks earlier were actually letters and numbers.

When I departed the optometrist's office I drove to a basketball game and met up with some friends. As I entered the gym my friends yelled for me to join them. I walked over to where they were and as I stepped up onto the bleachers my foot slipped because the step was steeper than it appeared. One friend who was also wearing glasses was astute enough to say, "It will be fine after a few days things will look normal and you will be able to judge distance and steps a little better. Seeing as good as we do takes some practice." She was right. 20/20 does take practice and some getting used to, and it works.

Enjoy the journey!

CONTENTS

20/20 LEADERSHIP LESSONS

Love
Faith
Righteousness
Strength
Patience
Determination
Desire
Sight
Demons
Pursue
Opportunity
Hiding
Build
Listening
Neighbor
Diversity
Trouble
Decision
Envy
Courage
Light
Nope
Reconciliation
Heartbreak
Plans
Bias
Past
Alignment
Rejoicing
Wholeness
Celebration
Nuts

THE FIRST CHAPTER

LOVE

FAITH

RIGHTEOUSNESS

STRENGTH

PATIENCE

Love

See what love the Father has given us, that we should be called children of God; and that is what we are. The reason the world does not know us is that it did not know him. Beloved, we are God's children now... -1 John 3:1-2a

"A spiritual partnership is between people who promise themselves to use all of their experiences to grow spiritually. They use their emotions to show them how to create constructive and healthy and joyful consequences instead of destructive and unhealthy and painful consequences." -Gary Zukav

Once, while visiting with a dear friend and her family, I noticed how much love, grace and patience with others, particularly children, can pay-off in the long run.

The couple has three little children, a boy and two little girls - twins. The little boy is at the age where he is getting into everything; he watches your every move and hears your every word. His eyes are big and beautiful and are filled with joy and wonder as he moves about the house.

I watched him pick-up his toys as he moved them from one room to the other – he was very careful with all of his items. Even when he approached the household cat and dogs, he was very gentle with them. At one point I said to the father, "He is very careful and almost nurturing with all of his things...even the way he interacts with the animals demonstrates some kind of affection and admiration."

The father responded, "It only works because the feelings are mutual."

It took me a minute to slip into reflective mode, but I did and I quickly realized that the little boy had figured out what many adults need to figure out – for love to be beneficial and efficacious it has to be mutual. Otherwise, we feel that we are taken advantage of or that we are wasting our time loving someone who will never love us back.

That little boy expressed his love for those animals and they expressed their admiration for him – their relationship worked beautifully. Just imagine the potential damage that could result if one, the boy or the animals, changed their opinion toward the other...disaster, disaster, disaster.

The thought of what this little boy is modeling for his younger sisters is also important. But, where did the boy learn this behavior? How did he figure it out?

Our parents, friends and general community teach us many things about how to be in harmonious relationships. Sometimes harmonious existence comes by way of silence and compliance and other times it comes as a result of open and honest communication.

When silence and complicit behaviors are favored or rewarded it teaches us how to be quiet and allow things to happen in us or to us that we may not appreciate. However, over time it becomes our norm and whenever we hear or see something contrary to our way of being we struggle to make sense of it and may even avoid it out of fear for what may happen to us if we act or respond that way.

Leaders are aware that love calls for action, communication, and expression of one's true self. Leadership calls for exploration of what it means to have voice and liberty in the world and in relationships. Love expressed by leadership in words and deeds never fails.

REFLECTION

How do you express love and compassion in your role as a leader? How do those you serve know you love them? Are the words you use and policies you uplift grounded in love? Would those around you know you love them if you never uttered the words?

PRAYER

God, you created me out of love, to love. Help me move beyond relationships that are not steeped in or built upon love. Help me give and receive love with gladness. Amen.

JOURNAL

Faith

Faith is the reality of what we hope for, the proof of what we don't see. The elders in the past were approved because they showed faith. -Hebrews 11:1-2 (CEB)

"I believe if you keep your faith, you keep your trust, you keep the right attitude, if you're grateful, you'll see God open up new doors." -Joel Osteen

When I was in college I was what they called a "starving student." I had to rely on God for everything. Things were so bad at one point that I went downstairs to get in my truck, which was on "E" to drive those 4 miles to school and found I had a flat tire due to a nail puncture. Under normal circumstances this would not have been a problem. I would have replaced the tire with the spare and moved right along. However, a week earlier I had to use that little donut spare and it was what was getting me to Friday.

I recall sitting there in the parking lot sobbing like a baby. I was scared, disappointed, and hopeless - you name it and I was it. Somehow I managed to drive that truck, with the flat tire to Big O Tire Center a few blocks away. I had gone through my sofa cushions, change cups and had scraped the floorboard of my vehicle and had gathered a whopping $6.35, mostly in pennies. I seemed to have recalled a $5 spare tire sale sign at Big O...I drove in there and told them I needed a $5 spare put on and they said, "Aight."

I sat there patiently, praying prayers of thanksgiving and singing little praises like, *"Great is thy faithfulness, great is thy faithfulness. Morning by morning new mercies I see. All I have needed your hand has provided. Great is thy faithfulness, Lord unto me."*

When the attendant came over and informed me that my truck was ready. I was getting ready for the embarrassing "clump" of all the pennies onto the counter when the man said, "That will be $18.20." He just as well told me the total was $5,678,234,987.19, because either way, I only had $6.35. So, I did what any other self- respecting person would do. I clumped my change onto the counter and I began to count, "One, two, three, four, five, six, seven, eight,..." and at about two hundred twenty-two, the man said, "Son, that one is on me."

Can I tell you that I suddenly knew what it meant to dance like David danced (II Samuel 6:14)? What a day and what a way for God to again lead me through that *valley of the shadow of whatever that was* to a clear place of light.

Service within the church context comes with many challenges. Some of the challenges are expected but there are others that come from out of nowhere. However, it is those challenges that come from out of the shadows that seem to do the most damage because those are the challenges that have been lurking all along and have not been called out or extricated from our existence. Sometimes those shadows are policies while at other times they are attitudes and customs that we know mean us no good. Yet, we live on as though they do not have any power to harm or to slow us.

It is the mighty presence and power of the Almighty God that steps in and shines light on all sides of what lurks around us to give us options to make different choices. When we are able and willing to choose what brings us into clearer view of God, then we show our faithfulness toward God. Strangely enough it is then that we also recognize God's faithfulness to us.

Since that experience, I have learned that in order for there to be shadows there must be light somewhere. Even if it is in the distance and cannot be seen by the naked eye it exists. Many things we see in life are mere shadows of true realities.

We do not see things as they are. We see them through lenses of fear and doubt that have been formed over time through disappointment and despair. Regardless of the extreme lack of clarity we have, light is the necessary element that brings all things into focus. That day in the tire store, God used that attendant as a source of light. The pennies clanging on the counter were shadows of a reality that lurked behind the eyes and in the heart of a man willing to be generous to a starving student.

REFLECTION

In what area of life and ministry are you struggling most to be faithful to God? In what areas of life or ministry are you most faithful and consistent? What supports you or holds you accountable to be faithful in life and in ministry? Where do you experience God's faithfulness to you?

PRAYER

Great Creator and Sustainer of the Universe, thank you for providing me with what I need to be successful in life. I ask you to continue to provide me with what I need to bring glory to you and joy to others. Use me where I am to be an instrument of light in the lives of others. Allow my presence and actions to call attention to how great you are and how marvelous life is in you.

When I focus on the shadows too long or allow them to become my reality, quicken my spirit and remind me that you are the source of light and you overcome all darkness in this world and in the one to come. Amen.

JOURNAL

Righteousness

To some who were confident of their own righteousness and looked down on everybody else, Jesus told this parable: 'Two men went up to the temple to pray, one a Pharisee and the other a tax collector... For everyone who exalts himself will be humbled, and he who humbles himself will be exalted.'

-Luke 18:9-14

"Earn the right to be heard by listening to others. Seek to understand a situation before making judgments about it."   -John Maxwell

Whenever the violent and destructive forces of hurricanes, tornadoes, wildfires, floods, war and terrorism ravaged places and people known to us there is a sense of indignation that looms around us. The images of families trapped on roofs, huddled in neighborhood centers, rushing to nearby public arenas and flagging down any moving vehicle that can take them to safety remain with participants and onlookers. Not only will those images leave an indelible imprint in the mind, they call our reason for existence into question.

We may never know the whole truth of who was to blame for the devastating aftereffects of the human induced traumas on society. However, as we continue to wrestle with what has happened to decimate ecosystems and annihilate once vibrant neighborhoods, we must remain mindful of two facts. The first is, finger pointing and name calling does not settle anything. In fact, such child-like behavior only serves to create greater divides and mistrust, which ultimately slows any potential progress.

The second is that now is not the time to decide who is/was right or wrong. Suffering is wrong and as many still suffer, that is where all of our support should be directed -- economically, physically, and prayerfully.

REFLECTION

As you contemplate your thoughts on the matter consider this: God is not concerned with who/what is right as much as God is interested in whom/what is righteous. When was the last time you insisted on being right only to realize that you had fallen short of being righteous in your pursuit? What does 'being right' satisfy in you? How does it feed your soul?

PRAYER

Lord, I want to focus more on being righteous and less on being right. Help me release my ego, my anger, and my pride. Amen.

JOURNAL

_____

_____

_____

_____

_____

_____

_____

_____

_____

_____

_____

_____

Strength

You gain strength, courage, and confidence by every experience in which you really stop to look fear in the face. You are able to say to yourself, 'I lived through this horror. I can take the next thing that comes along.

-Eleanor Roosevelt

My mom would often say, "Lord, give me strength" whenever she faced an obstacle or situation beyond her control. As a child I did not understand that prayer. Now, I do.

REFLECTION

As you consider what is ahead for you, your family, your team, and your vocation, consider how you will gain and maintain the spiritual and psychological strength needed to endure?

PRAYER

Lord, give us strength.

Give us strength to bring all our burdens and misgivings to you. Give us strength to hold on to the truths of your word until our change comes and your mission for us is fulfilled and your vision manifests.

Give us strength to let go of the things that keep us from growing closer to you. Give us strength to let go of the things that keep us from growing closer to others. Give us strength to clear our spiritual ears and to widely and unconditionally open our hearts.

We want and need all of these things so that we can become better acquainted with your voice. We want and need all of these things so that we can better acclimate to the direction you have charted for our lives.

Lord, give us strength to make it through this day and to experience at least one more victory that glorifies your name. Keep whispering to us, if that's how you are speaking to us. Keep shouting at us, if that's how you are speaking to us. Keep providing significant relationships in our lives, if that's how you are speaking to us. Keep us asking 'Are we doing to the right thing?' if that's how you are speaking to us. Keep speaking to us until we hear you clearly and follow you exactly as you command.

Lord, we know in our weakness, this prayer has already been answered. Amen.

JOURNAL

Patience

We are enlarged in the waiting. We, of course, don't see what is enlarging us. But the longer we wait, the larger we become, and the more joyful our expectancy.   -Romans 8:24-25 (MSG)

I was very busy one day. It was one of those days when I had twenty-six hours of chores and errands to complete in a six hour timeframe. As I started my trek, I was "moved" to swing through a McDonald's drive-thru for a quick breakfast.

There I was in that drive-thru line trying to figure out what to order. I eventually settled on the Sausage McGriddle®. After completing my cash for breakfast transaction I proceeded to exit the parking lot. A black Ford Focus had stopped in front of me. I was slightly bothered by this because I think it is rude to block the flow of traffic just so you can check your bag for order correctness before leaving the lot. That should take place before leaving the window. So, there I am with an attitude and my attitude got even worse when I realized there was a Honda Accord in front of the Focus.

What I saw was a man on the driver's side standing with one foot in and one foot out of the car, while talking to a man who had his hand inside the passenger window. I was so bothered by this nonsense. My Sausage McGriddle® was getting cold, so I honked my horn. When I did that the driver of the Focus stuck his head out the window and yelled back at me, "Oh! I'm sorry; we should get out and help those guys push that car." I was embarrassed. The man in the Focus thought my honk was a request upon him to help the guys with the Accord, when it was really my insistence that all of them get out of my way.

For most people anger and anxiety often blind us to reality.

14

Frustration and haste cause some to miss out on excellent growth opportunities. As leaders who can weather the storms riddled by anger and frustration, love and sure patience for humanity allows grace to look and mercy to wait. But be careful because it has been said, "God stores patience on the other side of Hell, so you may have to go thru Hell to get it."

REFLECTION

In what areas of your vocation and relationships are you in need of patience for those around you and for your self?

PRAYER

Patience, Lord. Grant me patience, I think. Amen.

JOURNAL

_____

_____

_____

_____

_____

_____

_____

_____

_____

_____

_____

THE SECOND CHAPTER

DETERMINATION

DESIRE

SIGHT

DEMONS

Determination

"A dream doesn't become reality through magic; it takes sweat, determination and hard work."
                                                              -Colin Powell

"Our greatest glory is not in never falling, but in rising every time we fall."

                                                              -Confucius

While waiting in a long line at the grocery store, I witnessed hope in action. Actually it may have been faith or just a wish that a stroke of good fortune would fall the way of the 10-year old boy who obviously had some financial backing for his project.

He was standing at one of those machines with the movable claw. He carefully inserted his bill and ever-so cautiously moved the arm over a Spider Man action figure and pressed the release. First try, no Spider Man. Second try, no Spider Man. Third try, he paused and walked around the machine to get a different view of his objective before trying again, no Spider Man. By now several other children gathered around in awe of what was taking place. The boy attempted a few more times, when suddenly one of the smaller children said, "Try something else!"

At some point in life and ministry every church and every church leader has had or heard an idea that just might have taken the church in a new or different direction. There were bright eyes and energy enough to sell the idea and there may even been a crowd willing to watch, but the meeting with the pastor led to a meeting with the Staff/Pastor-Parish Committee and that meeting led to a meeting with the Finance Committee, the Treasurer, the bookkeeper and her mother. That meeting led to a parking lot conversation about the new idea where you or the visionary felt inspired to stay the course even though it meant another round of meetings because there were no minutes taken the first time because the secretary never typed the minutes and/or there was not a quorum present so all they could do was talk without taking any action. When all the new idea needed was a group of children to gather around and say, "Try something else!"

After the boy tried a few more times for Spider Man, he moved the arm/claw over just a smidgen' and finally secured a Power Ranger. I am certain I then heard the boy exclaim, "I just wanted something good out of there!"

Sometimes we work to get the results we desire, with little or no result. We set in our mind that "this is it" and we move forward investing all the prayer, faith and resources at our disposal, when maybe our effort and intent are solid, but our actual goal or objective may be too much to bear. Or maybe our objective was set before us to get us in the vicinity of what we really need.

REFLECTION

What was your last goal you set that you did not reach? What did you learn about your self from the situation? Now that the experience of that particular experience is behind you, consider where are you investing your best energy, time, and financial resources? Who knows what you are working for or moving toward? Who is in your corner saying, "Try something else?" What is your own message to yourself about what you are determined to accomplish?

PRAYER

Lord, I have tried all I know to try. I have relied on the counsel of friends, the strength of prayer, and the truth that you know me and you want me to experience life abundantly. There have been options and obstacles that I have failed to access or to overcome. I tried and failed and at times I have failed to try. Forgive me, O Lord. Grant me a spirit of determination so I never give up on the vision you have of me. And so it is!

JOURNAL

_____

_____

_____

_____

_____

_____

_____

_____

_____

_____

_____

_____

_____

_____

_____

_____

_____

"Teams make you better than you are, multiply your value, enable you to do what you do best, allow you to help others do their best, give you more time, provide you with companionship, help you fulfill the desires of your heart and compound your vision and effort."

-John Maxwell

Desire

Take delight in the LORD, and he will give you the desires of your heart.
-Psalm 37:4(NIV)

"The key to success is to focus our conscious mind on things we desire not things we fear."
-Brian Tracy

Have you ever stopped to ask yourself, "Why me?" Usually we ask that question of God when things are spinning out of control; we feel as though we are out of control or have lost control. But how often have you asked that question when things are going well and on schedule? Everyone is falling in line the way you direct. The funds are streaming in as expected. Relationships are putting smiles on your face. You could not imagine life being any better than it is...but, have you ever stopped in the midst of all of that goodness and asked, "Why me?"

Within the congregational context, have you ever wondered why strangers visit the local church you attend? Do you contemplate why of all the churches in your area, they chose the one you also chose? Equally, do you ask the same questions when weeks have passed and there has not been a single new face? Do you squawk "why us" after several calendar pages are stacked on the floor and the baptismal font has faded into the hinder reaches of the chancel?

During the summer of 1996 (Atlanta Games), I served as a missionary in Botswana. It is a country the size of Texas with a population of 1 million in Southern Africa. That was an experience that forever altered my life and my self-perception. It was while in Botswana that I discovered that there was a discipline of study termed black theology. I also learned to play chess. I learned that there was a snake in existence that can make small dogs disappear in a matter of just a few minutes. I learned that cheese, when it costs approx. $9 per pound is a delicacy. I learned that it is possible to get a haircut, under a tree, with clippers powered by the barber's car battery/generator. I learned that children, no matter where they reside are open, loving, accepting and curious. I learned that God is at work in so many mediums, religious expressions and cultures, beyond my own. All of those things were keen insights or expressions that enhanced my experience.

However, it was when one of the missionaries shared a verse of encouragement with me and the other 3 members of my team that my eyes were truly opened. The missionary began with the other male on the team and moved on to the 2 women. I was last. Mind you, the other team members received those well-known, cool verses (Jeremiah 29:11, Isaiah 41:9-10, Romans 8:28) that anyone would love to have spoken into their lives. The verse I received, with many prefaces was Psalm 37:4. I must have looked at the missionary with a puzzled look because her response spoke directly to my confusion.

She said, "Don't worry about what you desire because God is the one who gives you the desires of your heart. But keep in mind that it comes as a result of you delighting yourself in the Lord." If what that missionary shared with me holds true, then as a leader within the church context and as a follower of Christ you have a responsibility to seek the desires God has for the ministry you have been called to serve.

REFLECTION

What does your heart desire? What makes your heart beat for the things of life and humanity? Where do you find delight in serving, giving and sacrificing? Consider what motivates and inspires you to do your absolute best and what hinders you from expressing what you want for yourself or from others.

PRAYER

God, let me come to know the desires you have placed in my heart. I want to rid all selfish desires so that I can be a person of faith – one who loves you with my whole heart. As you wash my heart and purge my mind, give me a drive to seek truth in your Word and find peace in your service. I desire to be a true worshipper. One who never doubts your presence or gives into the voices that speak loudly of your inadequacy and irrelevance in my life. I believe you are my heart's desire. And so it is!

JOURNAL

_____

_____

_____

_____

_____

_____

_____

_____

_____

_____

"If you're working on something you care about, you don't have to be pushed. The vision pulls you."

–Steve Jobs

Sight

We walk by faith, not by sight.   -II Corinthians 5:7

"The only thing worse than being blind is having sight but no vision. "

-Helen Keller

As I ran along the beach one morning, I noticed several interesting things. One thing I noticed was the lack of curtains on the windows of the homes that line the beach. Another thing I noticed was the number of individuals who were out there running, cycling, rollerblading and just sitting alone. Where had they come from and where were they going? What was the purpose of their presence in one of the most serene places in our region? An even better question: Why was I so concerned about their musings?

As I looked at various individuals I began to imagine why they would be out on a beautiful Tuesday morning, alone at the beach. Then I saw a man walking very slowly, alone with a cane. Surely he could find a sidewalk or a park close to his residence that would afford him ample walking space. I wondered why this man would struggle to cross the sand while walking with a cane when there were clearly easier routes he could have taken if all he wanted was some exercise.

I have no idea why that man *had* to cross the sand but it appeared for him this was his goal and his only option. I have no idea how long it's been since he last saw the ocean. I have no idea if this is a daily ritual that gives him reason to live. What I do know is that he made his way to the edge of the water and he just stood there looking out toward Catalina. He looked more than content with his position and his accomplishment.

As I watched him I realized, leaders cannot afford to let what we perceive keep us from moving onward, upward or outward. Leaders must tread around with the confidence that Christ provides, to be able to stand anywhere for as long as is needed - without falling short due to someone else's or our own perceptions.

REFLECTION

What are the hopeless images that cloud your mind and still populate your conversation? What are some possibilities you are aware of where you can be more loving and kind? What decisions must you make to move closer to the vision you have for your life and work?

PRAYER

Lord, help me see beyond the horizon that others have set for me. Allow me to experience true, loving relationships with family, friends, and strangers. Allow me to show mercy and compassion to those I know need it.

Grant me new challenges that make me better, stronger, wiser. I desire to be better than I have been. I admit I act like I have it all together and that I do no wrong. But, you and I know better. You know the truth that is locked deep inside of me. You know my fears and my anxieties. You know how much I doubt myself and how much I really doubt you. Forgive me.

Grant me additional chances to grow and to change. I want to be better, stronger and wiser in you, not of myself or in my own will. You are my God and I appreciate all that you do to keep me in this world, learning and loving, even with my limitations.

Thank you for your love. Amen

JOURNAL

_____

_____

_____

_____

_____

_____

_____

_____

_____

_____

_____

_____

_____

_____

_____

_____

_____

_____

_____

"Everything you've ever wanted is on the other side of fear."

–George Addair

Demons

"Man tells his aspiration in his God; but in his demon he shows his depth of experience."   -Margaret Fuller

"Too many of us are not living our dreams because we are living our fears."   —Les Brown

Psychologist, Author, and Speaker, Dr. Barry Hart shares a story centered in the Tibetan monk tradition where every five years the monastery opens the Room of 1000 Demons as part of their training.[1]

All of the candidates are brought to the exterior of the room and it is explained to them that inside the room there are 1000 demons and each them are aware of the candidate's worse fears. He writes, "For example, if you hate spiders, once in the room you'll find yourself among 1000 of the worst kind of spiders imaginable." Of course many candidates opt out of the experience and very few remain open to facing the challenge. Prior to entering the Room, the candidates are told to remember two things: 1) "None of the demons are real;" and 2) "Keep moving your feet."

This is exactly what many ministry settings present to us. We have fears of not accomplishing a particular goal, letting someone down or downright failure. Yet, there isn't very much evidence to back up the narrative we have on replay in our heads. We just know if we fail the proverbial bottom will fall from beneath our lives. We condition our families, our teams, our congregations, our communities and our selves to fear our fears at all costs. Our fears become the plumb line and measure

[1] http://ezinearticles.com/?expert=Barry_Hart

by which everything is tempered and measured. It seems a simple lesson and one that we know intuitively on some minimal level. However, we have often found ourselves facing fears and anxieties that lack a source in reality.

Some of those narratives and untruths include, but are in no way limited to: If we make this change people will be upset and they will leave; If we move that, then our biggest givers will stop giving; If we invite so and so into leadership it will alienate the Whomsoever Family; If we try something different and it fails we will never get to try anything new again.

The reality upon which they are based is someone else's reality. This is not to minimize physical danger or even psychological trauma inflicted upon us at some point. Those things happened and they were real. But, we are no longer in that same place.

We have other experiences and other relationships to factor into the equation. We have the option to stay where we are and continue experiencing the pain, fear and anxiety that has held us back or we can choose to keep moving – determining not to stay in a place where fear reigns supreme. We can choose to face our fears and eventually leave them behind. We can also choose to allow our past to dictate our future, while it diminishes our presence and impact in the world.

Prior to assuming a new leadership position, one of my mentors asked, "Do you have all your demons in order?" It was a curious but well-appointed inquiry. He told me that at any give time there are demons that lurk around every corner. When a leader's guard is down and ego is up, that is the opportune time for a purposeful demon to make a move that will seek to expose the leader's vulnerabilities by undermining the leader's integrity, confidence and reputation.

REFLECTION

What demons/fears would be in the room awaiting your arrival? What secrets to you have that help you harbor your demons/fears? What steps are you willing to take to diminish those demons/fears in light of the truth of the love and grace God has shown you?

PRAYER

Lord, have mercy. Give me strength to acknowledge my demons and to keep moving toward you. Amen.

JOURNAL

_____

_____

_____

_____

_____

_____

_____

_____

_____

_____

_____

THE THIRD CHAPTER

PURSUE

OPPORTUNITY

HIDING

Pursue

The goal I pursue is the prize of God's upward call in Christ Jesus.

-Philippians 3:14 (CEB)

"All our dreams can come true, if we have the courage to pursue them."

-Walt Disney

Sometimes when things were once novel to become familiar, they lose their flare and our attention often shifts to other places and things. That happens to leaders and to cherished things like an old doll, a collectible action figure, a favorite dress, lucky cap, special friends and former positions of authority.

A person stated, "I go to church almost every Sunday. I give an offering. I sing in the choir and I even usher and teach Sunday School when I have to. But, I just do not feel a connection to/with God. I try to read books to boost my spirit and to get me out of this slump, but nothing seems to work."

The person also shared that upon committing to be a follower of Christ the relationship was the priority of that person's existence. This new found salvation and freedom to love and to be loved was like a breath of fresh air. Now, that same relationship, with that same salvation and freedom seems burdensome and empty. That happens to many faith seeking people.

As the person poured out from the heart all that was in it, I was reminded of Apostle Paul's struggle to stay connected. He met opposition in many places and was ridiculed on every hand, but he knew that he had to do this one thing. This one thing would help him to prevail -- he had to keep pressing.

Pressing is like digging in, getting right next to, or even moving with force. Pressing is praying prayers and believing that God hears and answers them. Pressing is digging in your heels and daring the enemy to try to move your feet. Pressing knows that God is with you, even when you cannot muster up a feeling to contradict your current reality.

Leaders must "press" through the dry periods by praying for living waters to flow through the heart. Leaders must seek God to provide everything needed and consider what priority is placed upon the request. Those things God desires may only come to pass through perseverance. If a person or organization can obtain anything on it's own or of its own resource, then why request God's blessing or anointing in those endeavors? God is all sufficient.

When leaders surrender their will for God's will, their way may not be easy, but it will be overcome as they press their way with the faith and hope that God is with every leader who honors what God is doing and God will make a way out of no way.

REFLECTION

What are you pursuing or pressing for the sake of fulfilling your own life mission? What are you pursuing or pressing for the sake of your organization's mission?

PRAYER

Give me strength and courage I need to press on and to keep moving toward the vision you have for my life. When I am blinded by the light of temporary success, give me sight. When I am bound by my predictions and perceptions of others, give me liberty. When I am convinced that I am not as good as everyone else, give me a reminder that I am made in your image. When I am confused about my identity, give me a reminder that I am a beloved child of God. When I fear, fail and fall, give me another chance. Amen.

JOURNAL

_____

_____

_____

_____

_____

_____

_____

_____

_____

_____

_____

_____

_____

_____

_____

Opportunity

"Never lose an opportunity of seeing anything beautiful, for beauty is God's handwriting."   -Ralph Waldo Emerson

"The highest levels of performance come to people who are centered, intuitive, creative, and reflective - people who know to see a problem as an opportunity."   -Deepak Chopra

"We can easily forgive a child who is afraid of the dark; the real tragedy of life is when [women and] men are afraid of the light."   —Plato

I sat in a coffee shop waiting for my next appointment when I overheard a conversation between two women. One was a recruiter from a well-known business school and the other was a potential applicant. The recruiter told her, "Your credentials are impeccable. I appreciate you keeping this appointment, in spite of the bad weather we have been experiencing, but it shows me you are committed to your work and your education.

As the recruiter continued speaking, the candidate was rubbing her knuckles profusely under the table. The candidate was extremely nervous. Her nerves really got the best of her when the recruiter finally paused long enough to ask: "So, what other business programs have you applied to?" The candidate said, "Well, I uhm. I uhm...I applied to a couple local programs but that was really just to test the waters. Then I found out about how flexible your program can be, so I uhm...I decided to apply."

It wasn't the candidate's nerves, or the recruiter's tenacity that made this encounter memorable. It was the candidate's story that made it stick. After a few minutes of sharing in greater detail about the local programs she had applied to, she said, "As soon as I felt this program was the right place for me to be, things started to fall in place so it could happen. My husband works for the government, so prospects for him relocating from D.C. to Michigan were not in our immediate future without major sacrifice. However, I completed the application and continued praying about the possibilities. Then I learned of your visit to the area. The day I scheduled the appointment with you, my husband was granted a transfer to Michigan. With all of that, I know this is the right place and the right time. So, no matter how much rain was falling today, I was determined to keep this appointment."

The candidate went on for a while longer, followed by several exchanges with the recruiter. After the candidate was as candid as she was about her faith in the process and life, I was moved to tears. I thought back to times when similar things had happened to me and others, but I was also reminded of the many times that still, small voice had been silenced by reality and faithless chatter. In the context of ministry this happens with those folks who ask the questions that suck the air out of the room. Those who will not allow creativity to dark the doors out of fear they might lose a toehold on power in the church.

The recruiter shuffled through papers as they shared a little more. Then the recruiter said, "There were 5 other candidates who scheduled appointments with me for this morning, but all of them called, texted or emailed to say that due to rain, they would need to reschedule. I am impressed by your transcripts, work history and portfolio. I am also impressed by your story and your commitment, expressed by your presence here this morning...because you honored this appointment, I can guarantee your admission to the program."

You would have thought I had been admitted to the program the way my soul jumped for joy. There she was, as nervous as could be, but she was honest and committed before she entered the room. She did not shy away from the obvious hurdles of geography, personal financial challenges, her husband's employment, or the rain.

As leaders within our organization, we have to develop and encourage a similar work ethic and web of support when new ideas and initiatives are presented. We have to allow the Spirit to move the idea to where it needs to get. The same is true when we have new persons come into the church or join the committee. We must encourage inclusion more so than conformity because had this young woman conformed to the norm that where she was would be her life station for another season, she would have conformed the same way those other candidates conformed to what was happening in the moment versus looking beyond the horizon and trusting the rain was not the issue.

It was apparent she was a prayerful woman who had heard something deep within that gave her what she needed to pursue her dream.

REFLECTION

What opportunities are being blocked in your significant relationships? In your work or ministry? Where are you conforming a little too much? What or who influences or motivates you to conform when you would really like to make a different choice? What will it take to break free and give yourself and others permission to do something unlike anything you have seen before?

PRAYER

Help me, Dear Lord, as I seek to hear your voice and stay the course you have set for me. I pray that all chatter and clutter of my mind's eye and spiritual ear be replaced by markers of faith and peace as my soul says "Yes" to you and your will. Amen.

JOURNAL

_____

_____

_____

_____

_____

_____

_____

_____

_____

_____

_____

_____

_____

_____

_____

_____

"I want to be better.
You grow.
We all grow.
We're made to grow.
You either evolve or
you disappear."

–Tupac Shakur

Hiding

Living in the Most High's shelter, camping in the Almighty's shade, I say to the Lord, "You are my refuge, my stronghold! You are my God—the one I trust!."

-Psalm 91:1-2 (CEB)

We aren't like Moses, who used to put a veil over his face so that the Israelites couldn't watch the end of what was fading away. But their minds were closed. Right up to the present day the same veil remains when the old covenant is read. The veil is not removed because it is taken away by Christ. Even today, whenever Moses is read, a veil lies over their hearts. But whenever someone turns their back to the Lord, the veil is removed.

-II Corinthians 3:13-16 (CEB)

As a child, one of my favorite games was hide-and-go-seek. I loved to play this game because it required creativity, agility and speed. However, the only time I remember playing the game and truly enjoying it was when we visited Mrs. Kathleen. She had six or seven kids and there were plenty more in the projects where she lived. It was like one big happy family - kids were always around and there was always a big kids' game in progress. There were several good hiding places and plenty of room to run when you were trying not to be apprehended by the chasers.

One thing that sticks out in my mind now is that although I was hiding, I was never alone. At least I never felt alone. It's as though knowing other kids were around, was my refuge. It's as though knowing that someone was always going to be looking for me and would eventually find me was my source of comfort.

Yet, as leaders when we consider hide-and-go-seek in a spiritual context, there is another side of this analogy. Moses placed a veil over his face out of reverence for who God is. The

Israelites "put a veil over their hearts," according to the Apostle Paul, which keeps them from knowing Jesus as Lord.

Hide-and-go-seek is what leaders play with God when leaders try to pretend to be something that they are not. It is the game leaders play with each other when one appears or pretends to be on cloud nine, when hell is where most of our mail is delivered.

REFLECTION

What are you attempting to hide from God? What truths are you hiding from your closest associates? How much more effective would you be as a leader if you hid nothing from your team? Who do you trust with your truth? Do you have relationships that are based on consistent principles of confidence, transparency, and accountability? How different would your family, relationships, or organization be if you were a leader who did not hide any part of who you are or what you desire?

PRAYER

Lord, I hope you are pursuing me. I pray that you come and that you find me in my hiding place. Rid me of all that I use to hide myself from you and from the world. My soul hears you counting the seven days you took to create the world; the sixty-six books of the Bible you use to teach us; the forty-days Jesus spent in the wilderness you use to strengthen us; the three days he spent in the tomb you use to raise us up. My soul hears you counting so I can be ready to come out of hiding – in plain view of you and your creation – as you created me.

My soul hears you counting my sins as forgiven. My soul hears you counting on me to listen to you and learn from you. My soul hears you counting me as one in the number who will proclaim the triune God as my one and only God.

O God, I am coming out! Amen.

JOURNAL

_____

_____

_____

_____

_____

_____

_____

_____

_____

_____

_____

_____

_____

_____

_____

_____

_____

_____

_____

THE FOURTH CHAPTER

BUILDING

LISTENING

NEIGHBOR

DIVERSITY

TROUBLE

Building

It's like a person building a house by digging deep and laying the foundation on bedrock. When the flood came, the rising water smashed against that house, but the water couldn't shake the house because it was well built.

-Luke 6:48(CEB)

"Leadership is lifting a person's vision to high sights, the raising of a person's performance to a higher standard, the building of a personality beyond its normal limitations."
-Peter Drucker

"If you want to build a ship, don't drum up the men to gather wood, divide the work and give orders. Instead, teach them to yearn for the vast and endless sea."
– Antoine de Saint-Exupery

On an appointed Saturday morning while visiting Portland, Oregon and enjoying the finest accommodations, we found ourselves scrambling around the breakfast area trying to make a meal out of a sundry of items provided by the Best Western. Most of us clearly had early appointments or needed the first jolt of java, or both, so there was not much small talk taking place. Only a few mild grunts and half-hearted nods filled the crevices between the scrambling guests. Nevertheless, people were moving about with purpose, but not with extreme energy or direction.

The attendant was not yet fully prepared to receive the java zombies no more than she could pause to entreat those who were asking to assist her with her tasks. In the midst of the scurrying there came a faint voice from around the corner. It was a woman's voice, obviously of a certain generation. A voice from one of those generations that knows of rationing foods, stock market crashes, stratification of castes. One of those generations that knows what it is to be both Hatfield and McCoy, but do not care much for keeping up with the Jones's.

One of those generations that coined slogans for wars and rumors of wars, of men and women going off to quite possibly never return again. Those generations. But, that could be any generation since war and terrorism abounds, water is scarcely made available at the same time we are told the Earth may have too much of it to sustain life as we know it. Those generations. That was my thought as I heard a faint voice pierce around the corner, asking, "How do I get Channel 5? I want a local news station like the one I watch in Seattle...How do I find it?"

By this time I had made my way around the corner and caught a glimpse of this beautiful creation of the Almighty. She smiled. Yes, she was of one of those generations. As the television's volume increased, I said, "Looks like you got something there." She smiled and said, "Yeah, it's on but it's not the local news. The only thing here is something showing us how to build a house and it looks like a big house." I said, "That's something we need. We need to know how to build a house for all of us." She replied, "You're right and I believe Jimmy Carter tried to teach us that."

Building a house for all of us is what true leadership inspires because leaders who have a heart for serving people will do so in ways that allow others to see themselves doing something great for others.

Leaders listen. Leaders help. Leaders make room for others to lead. Leaders share what they have. Leaders give of who they are so others come to know who they can be, not so they can be like the leader, but so they can become leaders. That means leadership is more about inspiration of the whole than it is about aspirations of the one or of a few.

As I walked away I heard her telling others, "They are trying to show us how to build a house."

REFLECTION

What are your key leadership attributes? How do you know you are a leader? How do others know you are a leader? What qualities and characteristics of your leadership style inspires others to become leaders?

PRAYER

Dear Lord, I believe you created all that is and you decreed all of it, including me, good. I also believe you implanted leadership skills and characteristics in me. My prayer today is that you will stir up those gifts and use me to inspire others to do likewise. Amen.

JOURNAL

Listening

"A true leader has the confidence to stand alone, the courage to make tough decisions, and the compassion to listen to the needs of others. He does not set out to be a leader, but becomes one by the equality of his actions and the integrity of his intent."   -Douglas MacArthur

"The most basic of all human needs is the need to understand and be understood. The best way to understand people is to listen to them."

— Ralph Nichols

The wise hear them and grow in wisdom; those with understanding gain guidance.   -Proverbs 1:5 (CEB)

Some time ago I attended one of those high-price, very nice affairs. It was one of those white linen table cloth, fine silver and dazzling crystal dinners, with who's who of Los Angeles in attendance.

As I sat there observing the comings and goings of some of the City's elite, I noticed that there were some who never actually occupied a seat; they just kept walking around table-to-table, greeting everyone. One of those "floaters" eventually made it over to our table. As she approached our table, one of the women at our table became overly excited about seeing the woman.

The woman walked over, kissed the ecstatic woman on the cheek, and politely greeted the entire table. After a few moments one of the men at the table asked the *floater*, "Did you work for Northrop?" As she stood erect and lifted one arm above her head in a Bette Davis-like pose, she said, "Work? I don't work. I am an heiress!" Everyone laughed. The man, pointing to his girlfriend said, "She must also be an heiress. She does not work either!" The girlfriend looked stunned as she said, "I am not an heiress. I am a Scorpio!"

REFLECTION

Funny? Of course it is. How often have you heard what you wanted to hear? When have you answered a question that had not been asked or jumped to the wrong conclusion out of ignorance?

PRAYER

God, as I go through life, open my ears more and close my mouth even more often. Open my eyes more and close my mouth more often. God, open my plans, thoughts, senses and desires to what is right in you. Then, give me the words to speak, only if necessary. Amen.

JOURNAL

*"For few matters
you need to be solo,
for some matters
you need soul mate
and for many
matters
you need society,"*
–Amit Kalantri

Neighbor

The One of the teachers of the law came and heard them debating. Noticing that Jesus had given them a good answer, he asked him, "Of all the commandments, which is the most important?" "The most important one," answered Jesus, "is this: 'Hear, O Israel: The Lord our God, the Lord is one. Love the Lord your God with all your heart and with all your soul and with all your mind and with all your strength.' The second is this: 'Love your neighbor as yourself.' There is no commandment greater than these." -Mark 12:28-31

"From the equality of rights springs identity of our highest interests; you cannot subvert your neighbor's rights without striking a dangerous blow at your own." –Carl Schurz

I was driving hurriedly and ended up behind someone who was truly out for a Sunday drive. It seemed that everything was working in that person's favor. My first response was one of disgust because if that person had driven a little faster I would have also made the lights.

Well, as some Sundays go, I parked in a nearby parking lot, tended to my business and prepared to return home. Wouldn't you know it...that car that had caused me such grief was leaving that same parking lot, traveling in the same direction. Now I was really getting bothered. Was it possible that I could be hindered by the same car twice on the same day?

I meandered back along a side street behind the little white Honda. Whenever I needed to make a right, so did the Honda. The funny part of this is that when I signaled to turn onto my street, so did the Honda. Now I am really laughing.

When I signaled to make the necessary U-turn to get to my home, so did the Honda. Can you see me stuck somewhere in the middle of the twilight zone? The Honda made the U-turn and so did I. The Honda passed up two buildings and parked on the street. I thought, "at least you are not blocking my driveway."

I parked in my garage and as I walking up to my apartment I saw the woman as she yelled, "Hello! You must be my new neighbor. I was planning to stop by to introduce myself later today but since we are here...my name is Cheryl."

We stood there on the sidewalk exchanging niceties for a few minutes. I felt bad for thinking such horrible thoughts and for drawing such negative conclusions about this woman's evil plot to destroy me and my Sunday afternoon with her driving tactics. We completed our conversation and as I walked away I looked down and noticed that Cheryl was wearing a very large knee brace.

Of course I wondered why she would put herself in danger by driving in her condition, but then I remembered one thing Cheryl said during the course of our conversation. She said, "I just moved to California a few months ago and I do not have any family here." Here is a woman who is miles away from family risking her life and the lives of others to get a few items at the pharmacy, but I was so focused on my disgust that I completely overlooked any needs that Cheryl may have had or expressed.

REFLECTION

What kind of neighbor are you? Are you a 'neighborly' leader? How do you connect with those around you? How does your team know you will honor their ideas and protect them? What incentives do you have in place to insure your team will maximize their potential and their role in fulfilling the mission?

PRAYER

Dear Lord, help me to love myself and to cherish life so much that the mundane things of this life do not hinder me from also loving my neighbor. Help me to extend hospitality in this hostile world. Help me recognize what it must feel like to have to adjust to a new way of being – among strangers. And so it is!

You created us to be in community and to care for each other. You created us to love each other. In fact, as you spoke to your disciples at the Passover, you said, "they will know you are Christians by your love for one another." Your love is my love. My love is for my neighbors - all people. Amen.

JOURNAL

_____

_____

_____

_____

_____

_____

_____

_____

_____

_____

"An individual has not started living until he can rise above the narrow confines of his individualistic concerns to the broader concerns of all humanity."
— *Martin Luther King, Jr.*

Diversity

"Ultimately, America's answer to the intolerant man is diversity."
−Robert Kennedy

"Growing is the result of learning."   -Malcolm X

"You may not always have a comfortable life and you will not always be able to solve all of the world's problems at once but don't ever underestimate the importance you can have because history has shown us that courage can be contagious and hope can take on a life of its own."   −Michelle Obama

Therefore, as a prisoner for the Lord, I encourage you to live as people worthy of the call you received from God. Conduct yourselves with all humility, gentleness, and patience. Accept each other with love, and make an effort to preserve the unity of the Spirit with the peace that ties you together. You are one body and one spirit, just as God also called you in one hope.

-Ephesians 4:1-4(CEB)

Mainline denominations in the United States have struggled for many years to slow and turnaround the massive losses in church membership. Some denominations have concentrated their efforts in foreign countries and others changed their doctrinal stances to make it more acceptable for them to receive persons who would not have fit their target audience just two decades ago.

In my most recent pastoral appointment I was assigned to serve as Lead Pastor of what was labeled as a multi-cultural, multi-lingual, and multi-site congregation. It was all three plus twenty other labels that would work in defining this congregation. There were two campuses located 1.2 miles apart. On one campus there were three worshipping groups (English, Khmer, and Spanish) and on the other campus there were two worshipping groups (Tagalog and Tongan).

Prior to my arrival it seemed that in order to unify this

congregation we would need to begin worshipping together at once and dispense with all the culturally specific elements of these groups. You can imagine those discussions did not go very far and they were not well received. There were attempts to combine services and to eliminate some activities, but it was obvious that the more leadership tried to limit or prevent an activity, more activities sprang up and there was no end in sight.

One of the first commitments I made, as the Lead Pastor, was to build a pastoral and program staff leadership team that would function as one unit. We needed a unified leadership effort if we were to have any chance of creating a plan that would lead us to fulfilling a vision of a truly multi-ethnic and completely healthy congregation.

REFLECTION

As a leader in your context, imagine having to bring multiple groups and ideas together for a common goal. Do you have a scenario in mind? It may not be as complicated as what has been introduced here. It may be adding or canceling a worship service. It may be combining two Sunday School classes or moving three small group meetings from Tuesday night to Wednesday night. Where do you begin when you consider consolidating existing groups, activities or functions? What about that thought gives you anxiety? How could your anxiety be mitigated?

PRAYER

Creator and Sustainer of all that is and all that is to come. Give me a heart for all people in all stages of life. Allow me to accept those whom you accept and to release all the limitations I have placed on your love and willingness to include all whom you created. Amen.

JOURNAL

Trouble

Be happy in your hope, stand your ground when you're in trouble, and devote yourselves to prayer.   -Romans 12:12 (CEB)

When I was a child, one thing I hated hearing was "Boy, you are in trouble!" The announcement was usually NOT a surprise. I knew I had said, done or failed to do something. Maybe I had gotten "out of line" at school. Maybe I said a naughty thing on the playground. Who knows? I hated being in trouble.

Trouble always came with consequences. Trouble always seemed to linger. Trouble always, or at least the news of trouble, seemed to travel swiftly and often incorrectly.

What I find now is comfort in knowing that no matter who announces that I am in trouble, I am still a much-loved, cherished and protected child of God. Because I am a child of God, I know for certain that I am loved. I also know that "trouble don't last always" (I Peter 5:10).

Leaders and those whom they lead can claim to be a child of God and there is not anything anyone can do to change that. Each human being is created in the image of God and can strive to live into God's likeness. Think about it: Sometimes God [even] gets into trouble. People blame God for wars and for babies dying. People hate God when their parents get a divorce or a spouse is diagnosed with a terminal illness. People denounce their faith in God when natural disasters shake the social, political and spiritual fabric that has sustained individuals and communities for generations. Sometimes people will hate and despise leaders. They will not understand but God will. God always has and God always will understand the role leaders must fulfill in every situation.

REFLECTION

When have you felt God abandoned you? How did you reconcile what you believed about God and how you were experiencing God in your abandonment? Consider how you might lead others to realize the presence and power of God in each of their struggles.

PRAYER

Give me the courage to say "No" to the things that others want for me, so I might begin to scream "Yes" to the calling you have upon my life. Allow me to know that you are always with me and you understand my circumstances better than I ever will because you know and you crafted my destiny. Amen

JOURNAL

_____

_____

_____

_____

_____

_____

_____

_____

_____

_____

THE FIFTH CHAPTER

DECISION

ENVY

COURAGE

LIGHT

NOPE

Decision

"I made decisions that I regret, and I took them as learning experiences. I'm human, not perfect, like anybody else." -Queen Latifah

"Sometimes it's the smallest decisions that can change your life forever."

-Kerri Russell

Do you have a difficult decision that you need to make? If so, keep reading. If not, consider yourself blessed beyond belief.

I have discovered that difficulty around decision making is usually related to or the result of the mystery that surrounds the unknown factor imbedded within and around the decision. The "what if" game and the many in-head conversations you have with yourself that expose the litany of uninformed responses you may receive clouding the mind and blocking the heart from reaching any decision.

Here is something to think about: Do not let what you do not know determine your actions. Instead, allow what you do know to guide you. What is meant by that?

You know by now that God will never leave you and God will never forsake you (Hebrews 13:5). You should know by now that you have within you the very power that brought about resurrection on Easter morning. You should know by now that weeping may endure for the night, but joy comes in the morning (Psalm 30:5). Those are things you know and can depend on. What you may not know is *how* God will honor God's word and presence in your life.

With such understanding you should know comfort, security, joy, peace, help, hope, faith and a future are yours.

You do not know what you do not know, so go with what you

do know about the one who knows you best when facing tough decisions. The same is true in the church context as it is for your personal and social self. The familiar is comfortable and comforting even when we know it is not all it could be. We tend to accept the familiar and painful over the possibility that the new may be worse. Yet, imagining the new idea, option or choice brings about stress and anguish and eventually inertia takes up residence in our ministry setting. We often do not see it for what it is because the busyness continues, when all the while the business of the church is not being accomplished in His name.

REFLECTION

Where has God shown God's self to be faithful? When has God blown your mind with something new, different or unexpected? How did it feel when you were finally willing to let go of total and complete control of every aspect of your life and your future? At what point will you allow the presence and power of the Almighty to guide you to choose the righteous and unknown path over the legalistic and right path?

PRAYER

Lord, I know that you love me and that you only desire what is best for me. I ask you to help me grow in my understanding of you and your love. Also, help me to wait upon you to lead me because I do have desires in my heart and in my mind.

Some of my desires are spiritual aspirations, while others are material possessions, physical attributes and fiscal successes. Sometimes I know I am envious and jealous of others and what they appear to have. I struggle to see the many blessings I already have and the innumerable ones you have prepared for me.

Make me ready to give and to receive from a pure heart. May my intentions to please you be motivated by my love for you and what you desire to do in and through me. May I be attuned to your Spirit moving within me and prompting me to tap into what really connects me to you. As you delight in me, may I delight in you and the desires you deliver to my soul's opening. Thank you for hearing and for answering my prayer. Amen.

JOURNAL

Envy

Take delight in the LORD, and he will give you the desires of your heart. Commit your way to the LORD; trust in him, and he will act. He will make your vindication shine like the light, and the justice of your cause like the noonday.   -Psalm 37:4-6(NRSV)

"Success makes so many people hate you. I wish it wasn't that way. It would be wonderful to enjoy success without seeing envy in the eyes of those around you."   -Marilyn Monroe

Envy is a feeling of discontent and resentment aroused by and in conjunction with desire for the possessions or qualities of another. Envy is one of those subversive emotions or states of reacting or being that eats away at us and our relationships [sometimes] without us knowing it. Envy will sometimes cause us to demonize others and make close friends seem like enemies. Why? Because they have something we want and/or think we deserve. We often do not think the other person is worthy. If we did, we would congratulate them on their success and work toward fulfilling our own destiny instead of hoping to catch a glimpse of theirs.

The things you want for yourself or from others do not compare to the things God wants for you. The image you must use for comparison is not the one created by others. Look to the image God has in store for you.

REFLECTION

What is it about the way you were created that keeps you from being successful and believing in yourself? With whom or with what are you overly consumed that may be motivated by envy? What prevents you from having or being whatever it is that holds your attention in others?

PRAYER

Allow me to see my self the way you see me before I become blinded by what I want others to see in me. Give me patience and vision that will bring that version of me into focus when what others have and what others think clouds my field of view. I shall await the beauty that moment brings. Amen.

JOURNAL

_____

_____

_____

_____

_____

_____

_____

_____

_____

_____

_____

_____

_____

Courage

It is my expectation and hope that I won't be put to shame in anything. Rather, I hope with daring courage that Christ's greatness will be seen in my body, now as always, whether I live or die. -Philippians 1:20 (CEB)

"You gain strength, courage and confidence by every experience in which you really stop to look fear in the face. You must do the thing you think you cannot do." -Eleanor Roosevelt

January 2006, five months after the devastating and powerful waves and winds of Hurricane Katrina ravaged the coastlines along the Gulf of Mexico, namely Louisiana and Mississippi, I was in New Orleans for what was to be a festive occasion. Nearly a year prior to the Hurricane's arrival, the invitations to celebrate the nuptials of a friend and his bride-to-be had been delivered to a multitude of guests. On the beautiful spring afternoon that they visited St Patrick's Church and later engaged in cake tasting at a nearby hotel, they could not have imagined the future existence of either place would be in question between that day and the day set for them to pledge their lifelong love for one another.

On August 28, 2005, the Crescent City was in the path of one of the most destructive natural disasters in the history of the United States. That couple emerged from the storm having lost their home and a few possessions, but they still had each other and a pending wedding date. Some wondered if the wedding would continue as planned. Others knew with all the destruction, they would need to cancel their plans to be present.

After a few months the wreckage began to clear and the residents of New Orleans began to reclaim and rebuild their city as best they could. The couple opted to continue with the wedding as scheduled in January, five months after the storm.

There were thousands who were evacuated in the early days of the storm and many of them have yet to return. The reasons for their prolonged hiatus from the Crescent City are etched in economics, politics and the impact economics and politics have on the quality of life of the poor, marginal and vulnerable (former) residents. I saw them. I saw it with my own eyes.

Upon arrival in New Orleans and an eventual drive to a destination for custom haircuts and shaves, I saw them. As we drove down one particular street, things appeared in shades of grey. Not the in-between black and white grey, but that grey that comes from having pigment and filler fade. I saw what appeared to be a row of houses on stilts and the houses were grey. I saw women and men sweeping the porches and what had once been sidewalks and driveways. I wondered why they were sweeping incessantly, but my curiosity did not slow the sway of those brooms. My curiosity did not reimagine the color that once was – that is how deep the grey was on those houses and all that surrounded them. I saw it with my own eyes.

As we slowly made our way down that street and we began to make a right turn onto another street, I saw one splash of color out in the periphery. Amidst the deep, and certain greys that seemed the only reality those edifices and sweepers had ever known, I saw a leather turquoise chair on the porch of the corner house. The sure contrast between what this chair depicted and what was all around it captured my imagination but only for a millisecond because I quickly saw more as we turned the corner.

On that same block with grey upon grey and the turquoise chair on the porch of the corner house, I could see that some of what I had assumed were weather worn and storm damaged domiciles, were not at all as they appeared. Some were nothing more than frontal facades and what I saw were the remains of those structures and seemingly of those persons who once called them homes. I saw them sweeping and tending what was in hopes of what could be. The turquoise chair was a bright spot of color but it was not nearly as vivid as the hope expressed by those who swept those porches and places that were once sidewalks and driveways. I saw it with my own eyes and I felt it.

The bride was as beautiful as friends and family had imagined she would be. The groom was as joyful as any man is on the day he is betrothed the love of his life. The guests were there, ready and willing to celebrate and to support the happy couple, but there was something lurking in the background – the City and those residents who were not celebrating and those who were still wearing the label "refugee," whether in New Orleans proper or in distant U.S. cities that had granted them asylum and respite after the Storm.

I have returned to New Orleans several times since Hurricane Katrina. Once was while en route to help rebuild a home destroyed by her. However, each time I visit the Crescent City, dream of attending the Essence Festival, mention the sleeplessness of Bourbon Street, recall the budding jazz greats playing throughout the night, share Mardi Gras beads with total strangers, or desire to savor a hot beignet; regardless of where I am or the reason for the recollection of longing, none of those images or memories are ever as vivid as the image and motions of the sweepers who dwelled among the many shades of grey that served as background for that turquoise chair on the porch of what once was someone's home. I also know I saw it with my own eyes and I felt it in the marrow of my bones.

REFLECTION

What is your definition of courage? Consider a time when it seemed all hope was gone and no one could see or feel what you felt – a sense that you must "keep on keeping on" despite the physical evidence. How were you able to cast other's doubt and ridicule away?

PRAYER

Living God, often times I am without courage. I am without the will or stamina to rise above my own frailties and internal narrative that repeats in my head: "Who do you think you are?" Help me to acknowledge that I am your child and for that I am grateful.

JOURNAL

_____

_____

_____

_____

_____

_____

_____

_____

_____

_____

Light

"God saw how good the light was. God separated the light from the darkness.
-

-Genesis 1:4 (CEB)

"Men make history and not the other way around. In periods where there is no leadership, society stands still. Progress occurs when courageous, skillful leaders seize the opportunity to change things for the better."

-Harry S. Truman

I heard a comedian share once about being in a horrible situation. He had no idea how he would be able to pull himself together or to move beyond the mess he was in. He shared his plight with one of his closest and dearest friends. The friend offered a heartfelt, encouraging word. The friend said, "You've been dealing with this for a while. Can't you see the light at the end of the tunnel?" The comedian replied, "Yeah! But how do I know it is not a train?"

Sometimes we are so hard pressed with life and its issues that we are unable to even believe that there is a better, brighter or bigger "whatever" out there for us. But, that is a choice we make every day and in every situation. We determine how we will see the world and our plight. Jesus said, "The thief comes to steal, to kill and to destroy. I have come that you may have abundant life." (John 10:10). See, in that we already know the enemy's game plan.

We already know our outcome. So, we can choose to focus on what the enemy is doing with the killing, stealing and destroying or we can choose to focus on the abundant life that Christ offers. Does this mean that the killing, stealing and destroying shall cease? No. But what it does mean is that your energies will be focused on the things that will overcome the evil, versus allowing the evil to consume your time and energy. Leaders have a choice to believe whether the light at the end of your tunnel is the brightness of a new day or a train.

REFLECTION

Consider a time in your life and ministry when you believed the light at the end of the tunnel had to be train. How did your countenance change when you realized your service and even your anguish had not been in vain, but instead may have been what helped you hold out for the light of God to pierce through the darkness surrounding you?

PRAYER

God, give me eyes to see the bright future you have in store for me. Grant me a spirit of optimism when looking ahead. Help me rise above my own skepticism and cynicism so I might encourage others and myself. Amen.

JOURNAL

_____

_____

_____

_____

_____

_____

_____

_____

Nope

"The art of leadership is saying no, not saying yes. It is very easy to say yes."

—Tony Blair

Most leaders have sat through meetings that were scheduled for a set amount of time and just as the clock neared the appointed hour, the moderator attempts to cram a few announcements in to the final moments. It is a frustrating feat for the leader and for those held hostage in the setting. It seems every announcement is the most important announcement and every one who has one has to share it right now. That exact scenario happened recently and after about five such announcements and no end in sight, the moderator called to adjourn the meeting. As members began to push away from the tables and stand a man in the back of the room shouted, "Too bad you do not have room enough for farm workers!" I wondered why he did that. I wondered if there was some inherent bias in the room against farm workers that I somehow had missed.

Since that experience I have been extra sensitive to how announcements and varying perspectives are invited and introduced within various meetings and conversations. I have also noted how some information must also be excused. That is the more difficult thing to do because as a leader there is a duty of care and an expression of empathy and compassion that must be present so the work has integrity and can be unifying. However, when a leader fails to limit the unnecessary, the less critical and the non-strategic from the agenda or conversation, the necessary, critical and strategic slips from focus and becomes less attainable.

God has given you enough energy, resource, will, intellect and faith to accomplish what God desires for you to accomplish. You may not have all the energy, resource, will, intellect or faith to do what you want, but you do have what is needed to fulfill God's plan. Don't waste yours. Don't waste others' either.

REFLECTION

How do you feel when you have to say "no?" Why is it important to exhibit compassion and exercise discernment when chairing a meeting or leading a discussion? Is it ever acceptable to diminish the mission for the sake of not hurting someone's feelings?

PRAYER

Dear Lord, I am yours and you, I pray, are mine. Thank you for gifting me with all of the energy, resources, will and faith I need to fulfill the mission and live into the vision you have for me. Amen.

JOURNAL

THE SIXTH CHAPTER

RECONCILIATION

HEARTBREAK

PLANS

BIAS

PAST

ALIGNMENT

Reconciliation

"Christian faith is... basically about love and being loved and reconciliation. These things are so important, they're foundational and they can transform individuals, families."   -Philip Yancey

All of these new things are from God, who reconciled us to himself through Christ and who gave us the ministry of reconciliation. In other words, God was reconciling the world to himself through Christ, by not counting people's sins against them. He has trusted us with this message of reconciliation.

-II Corinthians 5:18-19 (CEB)

The woman walked in and cautiously scanned the coffee shop until she caught the eye of a man seated in the far corner. He sat there furiously reading over three pages of hurriedly scribbled writing on the pages of a crinkled spiral bound notebook. He was wearing favorably worn denim jeans and a nondescript blue t-shirt. The cap upon his head was certainly from his high school days of at least a decade ago. As he looked up from his notebook he saw her making her way across the floor and in his direction.

It was obvious from her attire that she has a high-powered corporate job by day or she likes to get it in with her girls at the local hot spot on Tuesday nights. Either way, she was absolutely stunning at six o'clock on a Tuesday. He saw it and this was not his first time beholding such exquisite beauty. Yet, what had been a very intense look at words scribbled on a page was transformed to a beaming smile that took control of his face as his eyes met her being. She was no stranger to what she saw either and her facial expressions told the full story as her smile turned to a grimace when he stood to welcome her. He extended his entire body to embrace her and she said, "Hello" as she took her seat without even brushing the back of his hand.

Someone who has never walked the path you have traversed can always find a reason or two to criticize your idea, your dream, your failure and your accomplishment. Everyone who has sojourned with you through the highs and lows will look upon you with amazement as you hold your head up high and refuse to be defeated. Anyone who believes or knows you were the impetus for their arduous journey or missteps may feel justified in seeing you struggle.

I am not sure which was the case for the couple in the coffee shop but I can imagine for him it may have been the "everyone," but for her it was most likely an "anyone" scenario.

As a leader you must be able to discern and to accept that church folks will undoubtedly show up in every category, and sometimes simultaneously. You may look upon a person with utmost respect and admiration in your heart only to receive a death stare or a less than hospitable greeting. You, like the man at the coffee shop may have a vision of reconciliation, but others, like the woman, may not be ready to embrace. The questions about humility, compassion, grace, mercy, retribution, retaliation, repentance, and forgiveness often surface when individuals or groups cannot or will not agree upon how to resolve an issue or conflict.

I tried to mind my own business and focus on my tasks but I was out of coffee and had nothing else to distract me from my work.

REFLECTION

With whom have you disagreed and wish to reconcile? With whom have you disagreed and do not wish to reconcile? With what do you struggle that prevents you from making peace with that person, group, or ideology?

PRAYER

Dear Lord, I pray for a spirit of reconciliation to be released in me and throughout my family, church and community. You have shown the most perfect example of how to love unconditionally and how to forgive those who sinned against you. Grant me mercy enough to arrive at a place in my being where I can release and reconcile with those who have sinned against others and me. Also, grant me grace enough that I may be fully reconciled within myself for the sins I have committed. Amen.

JOURNAL

Heartbreak

"Sometimes a little heartbreak is a lesson, and the best thing to do is just learn the lesson."

-Jon Voight

REFLECTION

Whenever you encounter a woman or man asking for financial help, what thoughts or judgments cross your mind? When you reflect on your own financial vulnerabilities, what does it bring to mind? Knowing that most people you see on a daily basis are no more than 1 paycheck and 2 decisions away from that same predicament, what are at least two stewardship decisions you will make for personally and professionally?

PRAYER

Lord, I want to cry my last tear today.

I am so sick and so tired of not knowing what to do. I just keep crying about how things are in the world. Then I cry about how things are not in the world.

When I think about the wars and the seemingly senseless killing that takes place around the world to fulfill ill-sought-after power or wealth, I cry. When I think about the children who spend their nights sleeping on the streets or sleeping in beds where men, and women alike, take advantage of them, I cry.

When I see mothers struggling to feed and clothe their children by means that pull her and the children farther into the gutter, I cry. When I see fathers finding importance in street credibility, I cry. When I see young girls fighting to be women and women fighting over a man, like young girls, I cry.

Lord, I want to cry my last tear today. For that to happen I think you need to show up in all these situations that I see on a daily basis. I want to cry my last tear today.

Is that possible? I believe you can do all things. Is it possible?

I suppose the problem here is that I will continue to cry until I truly realize that I can do all things through Christ who gives me strength to be present and active – working for liberation on behalf of all those who are oppressed and neglected.

Lord, I want to cry my last tear today, but knowing what I know...I need the strength that only you can give to allow me to continue this journey, with tears and full of hope. Amen.

JOURNAL

_____

_____

_____

_____

_____

_____

_____

_____

_____

_____

Plans

"The plan is nothing; the planning is everything."   -Dwight Eisenhower

"Plans are only good intentions unless they immediately degenerate into hard work."   -Peter Drucker

If a leader simply makes plans and never implements them, then the leader runs the risk of placing projects, teams, and organizations in a perpetual holding pattern. Plans can only be deemed valuable or useful after they have been implemented and evaluated. We have no way of knowing if driving directions will actually lead us to where we want to go if we never activate them, get in the car, and start following the directions.

I realize that sometimes it is scary to think about striking out in a new direction or starting a new venture. At some point you have to move beyond the imaginary to the experiential (living and doing what you intend and hope to do). The latter requires faith, the former breeds apathy and limits the confidence a leader needs those who follow to have in what is happening. Being able, willing and courageous enough to devise, disseminate and shepherd a plan from a thought to manifestation is something few can honestly place on a résumé. Owning what was created, succeeded and what failed also required of leaders. However, a big dream begins with a plan wed to courage. Vision comes in the dreaming that takes place beyond the doing.

REFLECTION

Are you dreaming big dreams, living out of your giftedness to achieve the greatness God desires for you? Do you envision

yourself in places doing things you never thought possible? Remember: planning is only one of many steps of this marathon called life.

PRAYER

Lord, help me to take my eyes off of others' prizes. Center my focus on what you have for me. Grant me the strength and courage to accept what is mine and to work to attain what you have for me. Also give me courage to share the plans you have placed within me. Give me someone to share with so I can be held accountable to someone other than myself. I shall await whomever you send and shall receive them with open arms. Amen.

JOURNAL

_____

_____

_____

_____

_____

_____

_____

_____

_____

_____

Bias

"Fortunately for serious minds, a bias recognized is a bias sterilized."

- Benjamin Haydon

"Our lives begin to end the day we become silent about the things that matter."   -Martin Luther King, Jr.

There was a woman who boarded a bus carrying a laundry basket with neatly folded laundry. She in the first vacant seat and it was next to man whom she did not know. After few minutes the man asked her if she would give him a cigarette. She responded, "You don't ask any help from me as a man! You can take good enough care of yourself." He seemed dumbfounded that she would offer such a harsh response. Others on the bus offered quiet and uncomfortable laughter. I must admit that it was borderline comedic to see this man cower at the sound of this woman's voice. However, the lesson here is far more impactful than the words she used. It was her bias and her filter that allowed her to quickly establish a boundary that she would not cross.

As a leader it is imperative that boundaries are established and maintained. It is also helpful to be able to identify biases that support or negate such limits and exceptions. A leader's consistency and sense of honor and integrity will be closely linked to the leader's understanding of boundaries and biases.

The woman on the bus had a bias about men and their ability to care for themselves and that assisted her in establishing her boundary that would not allow her to see herself supporting a man. It can be assumed, based on her words, that she would think it acceptable for her to ask the man for a cigarette. That may or may not be the case. Yet, the lesson here is that biases we bring into our relationships and service roles impact the boundaries we are willing and able to maintain.

REFLECTION

When have you struggled with setting good boundaries with another person? What biases can you identify that were involved in that situation? Are you in a better space where you can recognize when you are teetering on the margins of what is acceptable to you?

PRAYER

Almighty God, I know I have crossed some boundaries in my life. I have not always been aware of my biases and how they affect the way I show up in the world. Hold up your mirror to me and let me see the better way to protect myself and to guard the gifts you have invested in me. Allow me to bask in your presence and grow in your grace with gratitude. And so it is!

JOURNAL

Past

But she came and knelt before him. "Lord, help me!" she said. He answered, "It is not fair to take the children's food and throw it to the dogs." "Yes, Lord, but even the dogs eat the crumbs that fall from their masters' table."

-Matthew 15:25-27(NRSV)

In some ways, what you just read were scenes or acts that lead up to the climax or conclusion – it is what hooked you in, captured your imagination and kept you there until the end. At least that's how it happens with television and movies. Even in our lives sometimes we are captivated by our own or even other's past. We focus so intently on the past that it can keep us from seeing what we really want to see - the climax, the rescue, the plot twist, etc.

For the hope filled leader life is like a show you have waited a long time to see that is different from what you expected, but you keep watching in hopes of a happy ending or a thrilling plot twist. There is an unrelenting hope that "this too shall pass" and "joy will come in the morning," that reverberates in our souls. [And] there are those who will take every opportunity possible to recall the not-so-distant past mistakes or scandals that may or may not have been true. Then the wrestling and questioning sets in about the leader's qualities to lead or to even be one in the number. The happy ending may be coming but it is far from the ongoing nightmarish reminder of what once was.

What Jesus demonstrates and what leaders must accept is that the past is the past and it is what God will use to formulate your path and fortify a passion for your purpose. No reruns. No OnDemand. No need to TIVO.

You will be around for the highs and the lows, but know "this too shall be a part of your past."

REFLECTION

What leadership challenge have you faced that was difficult for you to navigate because of a past mistake or indiscretion? Have you forgiven yourself for what you caused? Have you forgiven others who will not let it or you go?

PRAYER

Lord, help me see others as you would have me see them. Also help me to see myself in a more positive light so I can vision past my own and others' pasts. I long to experience spiritual transformation in myself and in the lives of others. I am willing to let you lead me and guide me in your Word, your Work, and your World. Amen.

JOURNAL

Alignment

"Good leaders organize and align people around what the team needs to do. Great leaders motivate and inspire people with why they're doing it. That's purpose. And that's the key to achieving something truly transformational."

-Marillyn Hewson

"The way to achieve your own success is to be willing to help somebody else get it first."   -Iyanla Vanzant

I was minding my own business while dining in Denny's when I *managed to overhear* a conversation take place at a nearby table. There was an older, rugged looking gentleman seated at a booth. As a tall, slender, well-dressed man passed the booth the rugged man asked, "Can you give me some money to get something to eat?" The tall man replied, "Sure. How much do you need?" He replied, "Just a few dollars - just enough for some food."

The two men engaged in idle dialogue for a few minutes and the man eventually passed some money to the other man. I heard words of thanksgiving being shared. However, as the waitress passed their table the tall man stopped the waitress and asked for a menu. He said, "My friend here needs a menu so he can order? The rugged man said, "Naw! I don't want to order. I'm gonna take this money to the grocery store and get some food. The tall man said, "Why would you do that? There is food here." The rugged man responded, "I'm gonna go to the grocery store?" The tall man, very sternly stated, "I know one thing; you gone eat in this restaurant right now, or you gonna give my money back."

The rugged man ordered a Creole Skillet, passed the money to the waitress and thanked the tall man for helping out. The tall man left the restaurant.

As a leader within an organization known for benevolence it

can sometimes be difficult to discern what a person's true needs and intentions are, but that may not be the point either. Leaders have to lead with the vision in sight and the mission in mind. It is the values of the leader and the organization that guides the right actions.

REFLECTION

Do you find your core values are in alignment with your organization's core values? Are you clear about the vision? Is it easy for you to share the mission and encourage others to understand its importance to those charged to carry it out?

PRAYER

God help me to be a cheerful giver when I have gifts to share.

Help me to be a grateful and gracious recipient when gifts are offered or presented to me. May my values and judgments align with yours in every situation. Just as I receive your love and grace, I want to freely extend it to others without pause or conditions. Amen.

JOURNAL

_____

_____

_____

_____

_____

_____

_____

THE SEVENTH CHAPTER

REJOICING

WHOLENESS

CELEBRATION

NUTS

Rejoicing

Rejoice in the Lord always: and again I say, Rejoice. Let your moderation be known unto all men. The Lord is at hand. Be careful for nothing; but in every thing by prayer and supplication with thanksgiving let your requests be made known unto God. And the peace of God, which passeth all understanding, shall keep your hearts and minds through Christ Jesus. Finally, brethren, whatsoever things are true, whatsoever things are honest, whatsoever things are just, whatsoever things are pure, whatsoever things are lovely, whatsoever things are of good report; if there be any virtue, and if there be any praise, think on these things.   -Philippians 4:4-8*

"We are shaped by our thoughts; we become what we think. When the mind is pure, joy follows like a shadow that never leaves."   -Buddha

The Apostle Paul was no stranger to adverse situations and chaos seemed to follow him or precede him everywhere he traveled. However, throughout the Pauline texts of the New Testament, we find him encouraging the Saints to be thankful and to rejoice always. What does he mean? How is this possible?

"Be glad" or "rejoice" means to express joy over and over and over and over and over...It does not refer to being perpetually happy. Happiness is the result of an external stimulus or happenings that make you respond positively. Joy is the result of an inward working that cannot be explained, except that joy is not determined by external circumstances or stimuli. Joy comes from God, through the Spirit.

Joy comes when we know we are doing the will of God. Joy comes from us doing the work of the church. Happiness is an emotion we feel when we do church work. It is incumbent upon church leaders to know the difference between church work and work of the church and to help others focus more on the work of the church – the soul reaching, soul saving, soul nurturing activities and actions that cause the church to increase in faith and fruit each day.

Serving the homeless, praying with the sick, visiting those who are homebound, teaching a child to read, encouraging a teen mother to complete her education, welcoming a person freed from prison back into the community, helping young boys develop a trade or skill to get a job, giving to the family at the freeway ramp *just because*, packing and shipping cookies to soldiers on the battlefield, discerning a vision for the ministry, staying the course with the mission of the church, upholding the established values and passing them along to other generations for the sake of them embodying them and allowing them to be reshaped over time are but a few examples of work of the church. Church work is spending too much time figuring out how any of those things will or will not get done versus doing them.

REFLECTION

What were you doing the last time you felt you were happy? What were you doing the last time you experienced pure joy? What was different about those experiences?

PRAYER

God, I have heard that "the joy of the Lord is my strength." If that is so, why do I feel so weak? Why am I not filled with joy? I feel stressed and anxious on occasion. I find it difficult to smile when all is falling apart around me. I see others going about their lives with mountains of problems surrounding them but they do not seem to be as bogged down or as bothered as I am.

I have known happy moments and I want to believe I know what joy is, yet I cannot always claim it to be so. May your grace abound toward me so much so that I obtain great unspeakable joy that can only come from being in relationship with you.

Make my heart glad with thoughts of you. Make my life whole as I devote all I am to you. Make my soul secure by filling it with joy and sealing it with grace. Amen.

JOURNAL

_____

_____

_____

_____

_____

_____

_____

_____

_____

_____

_____

_____

_____

_____

_____

Wholeness

"Pay mind to your own life, your own health, and wholeness. A bleeding heart is of no help to anyone if it bleeds to death." -Frederick Buechner

Two long-time friends accompanied each other to a local clinic for their bi-annual HIV test. One of the young men was always afraid of a positive diagnosis, while the other felt his presence there was more for moral support than for the test. Well, this particular trip yielded information that neither was prepared to hear. The one who was always terrified left the clinic with his normal *negative* diagnosis. The other departed with a piece of paper and several pamphlets that confirmed his *positive* status.

REFLECTION

What thoughts, ideas or biases do you carry with you into a hospital room to visit a sick friend? What prayers do you pray for those around you who live in fear and in shame because of the dis-ease and disease that ravages their minds, bodies and souls?

PRAYER

God, it has been said that when we are sick, we shall call on the elders and they will anoint with oil, pray the prayer of faith and the sick will recover. You said in your word that by your stripes we are healed. You said in your word that you withhold no good thing from those who walk upright.

You may have noticed that I know what your word says. I know that there are promises of wholeness and healing in your Word. The problem here is that I have figured out how to get the words off the page and into my head, but I have not gotten the word from my head into my heart. I do alright assuring others of their success, salvation, healing and deliverance, but I fail miserably at affirming my own faith of a brighter today and hope for tomorrow.

I want desperately to believe that you will heal. I want desperately to believe that you will touch his body, his heart, his mind, and his soul and you will take the pain and the doubt away. I want to be able to lay my head on the pillow and know within my heart that you have me in the palm of your hands. That's what I want.

I need to let you hold me and to trust that what I perceive as inactivity, could be your way of waiting for me to be still and know that you are God.

Heal all who are wounded, broken, sick, abandoned, ashamed, scared and sacred. As only you can. And so it is!

JOURNAL

Celebration

So pay everyone what you owe them. Pay the taxes you owe, pay the duties you are charged, give respect to those you should respect, and honor those you should honor.   -Romans 13:7(CEB)

"It is better to lead from behind and to put others in front, especially when you celebrate victory when nice things occur. You take the front line when there is danger. Then people will appreciate your leadership."   -Nelson Mandela

I walked into the pastor's office and it was apparent that he had either bought a considerable amount of stock in a party supply store or there was a major celebration in the making. I inquired about the mounds of streamers, balloons, cards, and certificates. The pastor told me the supplies were for the many graduates they would honor the following Sunday during worship.

The church's average worship attendance was about 60 on a good Sunday, so the amount of supplies was disproportionate to the number of "graduates" one would expect from a congregation of its size. After deeper conversation and engagement, the pastor informed me that they celebrated every graduate associated with the Church from preschool thru graduate school. I said, "I don' t understand why you would honor kids for doing what they are supposed to do." From the recesses of the office the pastor's wife commented, "Well, everyone likes to be celebrated sometimes." I hung my head in disgust for how I had approached the situation and for the shortsightedness I displayed with my callous and inconsiderate remarks.

Every leader must consider how to reward and inspire the team and any would be followers. Individuals who willingly volunteer their time, talent, money, influence, and network to advance the mission of the organization or to ensure successful completion of a project must be shown appreciation. Most people who opt to give through volunteerism do not expect to be celebrated or rewarded for what they have done for others. However, when they are celebrated it raises the stakes and improve the attitude for everyone involved. This is true no matter how big or small the contribution or whether is routine, first time or repeat gift.

REFLECTION

Who have you failed to celebrate? How will you reward a volunteer or supporter so that they reap at least that benefit for their altruistic efforts?

PRAYER

O God, I shall give and know it will be given back to me. I shall love and know love will be forever mine. I shall extend grace and know even better what it is to receive mercy, always. Amen.

JOURNAL

_____

_____

_____

_____

_____

_____

_____

_____

"The most common way people give up their power is by thinking they don't have any."

— *Alice Walker*

Nuts

"Shallow understanding from people of good will is more frustrating than absolute misunderstanding from people of ill will." -Martin Luther King, Jr.

While visiting Portland, Oregon, I noticed several people carrying pink boxes with an interesting script and picture. Whether I was in downtown, on the train or near the Convention Center, I saw them throughout the city. Eventually I mustered up enough courage to inquire about the boxes and their contents. What I was told was a tale of a famous and popular doughnut shop that makes exotic flavored doughnuts.

On my last day in the city I boarded a city bus to take the 35 minute ride from my hotel to the nearest Voodoo Doughnuts location. While on the bus I noticed the area of town I was in was not as eclectic and as hip as the neighborhoods I had visited in other parts of the city. At one stop a man got on and sat in the middle of the bus. He surveyed the passengers and zeroed in on me. I braced myself for some outlandish chatter, but to my surprise the man made a single statement, "I wish I could afford a double burger." After making his statement he made idle chitchat with a few other passengers until a gang of four seemingly elderly men boarded the bus and sat across from him.

Once again, he surveyed the passengers on the bus and zeroed in on me. I braced myself for some outlandish chatter, and to my surprise the man asked one question, "Anyone have a cigarette I can buy?" The four elderly men laughed in unison and that drew the attention of the man who wanted a double burger and a cigarette. He seemed furious but he did not address the men. He continued looking around the bus and out the window as though he had lost something.

As the bus approached an assigned stop, the four elderly men stood to make their way to the rear door. One of the men had a jacket that brushed the side of the burger and cigarette man. They exchanged heated and harsh words with one another until the men had disembarked the bus. Then, the man surveyed the passengers on the bus and zeroed in on me. I braced myself for some outlandish chatter but to my surprise the man only had one question, "Can't he see I'm freaking disabled?"

I pretended to ignore him again in hopes that would remedy his curiosity, but I failed. I know I failed because as the man continued to survey the passengers on the bus and I braced myself for whatever, I noticed we were approaching my stop. Finally I would be able to enjoy some of those Voodoo Doughnuts. I would have my own pink box to carry back to my hotel. Just as I stood to make my way to the rear door the man said, "Hey!" I braced. He continued, "You can't be nuts in this town."

It would be mighty Christian of me to tell you I then paused and prayed with this man and shared my testimony, but that did not happen. I disembarked the bus, stood in an extremely long line, realized it was a cash only establishment, shortened my order from six doughnuts to three, got them, bought a t-shirt and walked back across the street to catch the bus back to my hotel. As I waited for the bus I questioned whether or not it was in my best interest to ride the bus or to take a taxi.

REFLECTION

Who do you avoid when you are out and about? What story of liberation and acceptance would you share with a stranger, if given the chance? How are you showing up in the world as your absolute best self? Do you ask for what you want? Are you sure of what you are about in every arena of life?

PRAYER

Jesus gave of himself so that all would have life and be able to experience life in abundance. May my heart open more and more each day so that my mind will be renewed each day. Allow me to see myself in those whom society has shunned and the church has excluded from its liturgy and its acts of charity. Use me to bring clarity about who Jesus is and what Jesus does in the hearts and minds of those who seek to be like him. And so it is!

JOURNAL

_____

_____

_____

_____

_____

_____

_____

_____

_____

EPILOGUE

As I approached my fourth and final year in the United States Air Force, I applied to Colorado State University in Fort Collins, Colorado. I did so because the school and city were within commutable distance of Cheyenne. I had found a church I liked with people who cared deeply for my spiritual wellbeing. As I applied for college the whole church began to pray that I would be accepted and that I would receive a sizeable scholarship. We also prayed that I would receive an early release from the Air Force because at the time there was a freeze on discharges due to the military build-up for Desert Storm – the first Gulf War. After a while we expanded the prayer list to include that I might get a good paying job and secure a place to live. It took some time but eventually answers to those prayers began to appear.

The first answer came as I received my acceptance letter from the Admissions Office and a clearance to enroll in the Occupational Therapy Program. The second answer came from the Air Force when I was approved for early release so I would have time to out-process and transition to Fort Collins before I had to start classes. The third answer came when I was awarded a sizeable scholarship and preference points for an on-campus job, with benefits.

Another answer came when I was informed there was space

available in a dormitory that housed non-traditional aged students. The church was so elated that God had moved so mightily and had granted everything on our prayer list concerning my transition from airman to civilian.

About four days before I was to move from Warren Air Force Base to my dorm room in Fort Collins, I began to get rumblings in my spirit that seemed to be telling me to "go home." I was confused because I did not have time or money to "go home" before time for me to report to work and start classes at Colorado State. The word and unction increased by the day until I finally gave in to what I believed the Spirit prompted me to do. I had to go tell my pastor and the congregation that after all of that prayer and celebration, after all that we had believed God had provided, I was to walk away from it all. I was to return to Alabama without a vision, plan or prospects.

It would take me nearly two years before I would catch a glimpse of what God was working together for my good. When it was all said and done, this was the third distinct time I could recall that my ability to sense, hear or discern what the Spirit was urging and my willingness to follow it put me on the right path. The first was when I chose to attend Danville School when my parents divorced. The second was when I saw Staff Sergeant Thomas McRae in his crisp blue Air Force uniform and knew I wanted to do whatever it was that he had done to be able to present himself the way he did at our school assembly. The third was when the Spirit uttered, "Go Home!"

The promptings of the Spirit have not always been so pronounced, nor have I always recognized such promptings in

advance. Most recognition has been in hindsight – when I look back I can see and hear what had happened to move me along. I can see those opportunities that challenged me to exercise self- leadership by making a decision to move from where I was regardless of how comfortable or conventional it may have seemed. It was a sobering feeling to inform an entire faith community that we may have somehow missed God along the way to trying to get what we wanted.

In hindsight, I do not recall a prayer of discernment about what the grand plan for my life might be. No, I wanted to stay close to my church family and they wanted me there so we did what church families do. We made our requests known and expected God to fulfill our desire instead of seeking the vision God had and then following that with a plan for how to live into it. We focused on what we wanted because there was not a clear vision out before us.

The 20/20 experiences are the ones that pack much power and those are the ones that have instilled the greatest desire to listen for the Spirit and to seek a vision that is far beyond where I find myself because those seem to take me and those sojourning with me closer to the divine and closer to each other. My hope is that the vision leads me as I lead others to be inspired by and in awe of what is set before us.

For You

If you would like to explore more about 20/20 Leadership Lessons and how you can incorporate and share these principles with other leaders and with your team, go to: www.leadershiplessons.org

For Your Team

If you would like to enlighten your team on the principles that you are exploring and imparting, invite the team to complete this exercise. You may order additional copies of this book at: www.leadershiplessons.org

For Your Organization

If you would like to discuss 20/20 Leadership Lessons with Dr. Bridgeforth or if you would like to schedule an in-person consultation or workshop, go to: www.leadershiplessons.org

For God's Glory

If you would like to glorify God through your service, be the best leader possible by imparting a vision, trusting reality and inspiring others to lead.

And so it is!

NOTES

Translations of the Bible

CEB   Common English Bible. © 2010, by the Christian Resources Development Corporation in the United States of America. All rights reserved.

KJV   King James Version. Public domain.

MSG   The Message. © 1993, 1994, 1995, 1996, 2000, 2001, 2002. Used by permission of NavPress Publishing Group.

NIV   New International Version. © 1978, by Zondervan in the United States of America. All rights reserved.

NRSV   New Revised Standard Version. Scripture quotations, unless otherwise noted, are from the *New Revised Standard Version*, copyright © 1989, by the Division of Christian Education of the National Council of the Churches of Christ in the United States of America. All rights reserved.

Additional materials

Most of the leadership quotes within this volume were listed by Kevin Kruse, Contributor to Forbes Magazine (2012).

Disclaimer

Names of individuals and companies have been changed as much as possible, so as not to draw attention away from the crux of the story and to avoid instances of liable, slander or breaches of confidence.

ABOUT THE AUTHOR

Dr. Cedrick Donyat Bridgeforth was born in Decatur, Alabama. He received degrees from Pepperdine University (Doctor of Education in Organizational Leadership), Claremont School of Theology (Master of Divinity) and Samford University (Bachelor of Arts).

Prior to beginning his career in nonprofit and church leadership, he served four years in the United States Air Force. Cedrick is a coach, consultant, educator, an Ordained Elder in The United Methodist Church, Director of Academic Programs and Outreach at the Ecumenical Center for Black Church Studies of Southern California at the University of La Verne, and a member of Alpha Phi Alpha Fraternity, Inc.

You may access more information about Dr. Cedrick Bridgeforth, other writings, recordings and 20/20 Leadership at: www.cedrickbridgeforth.com.

Made in the USA
San Bernardino, CA
13 July 2017